BOWIE

BOWIE

CRITCHLEY

OR Books

New York · London

Illustrations by Eric Hanson

Published for the book trade by OR Books in partnership with Counterpoint Press.
Distributed to the trade by Publishers Group West

First trade printing 2016

Cataloging-in-Publication data is available from the Library of Congress. A catalog record for this book is available from the British Library.

ISBN 978-1-944869-14-4

This book is set in New Caledonia and Alternate Gothic. Design by Bathcat Ltd.

10 9 8 7 6 5 4 3 2 1

CONTENTS

MY FIRST
SEXUAL
EXPERIENCE

LET ME BEGIN WITH A RATHER EMBARRASSING confession: no person has given me greater pleasure throughout my life than David Bowie. Of course, maybe this says a lot about the quality of my life. Don't get me wrong. There have been nice moments, some even involving other people. But in terms of constant, sustained joy over the decades, nothing comes close to the pleasure Bowie has given me.

It all began, as it did for many other ordinary English boys and girls, with Bowie's performance of "Starman" on BBC's iconic *Top of the Pops* on July 6, 1972, which was viewed by more than a quarter of the British population. My jaw dropped as I watched this orange-haired creature in a catsuit limp-wristedly put his arm around Mick Ronson's shoulder. It wasn't so much the quality of the song that struck me; it was the shock of Bowie's look. It was overwhelming. He seemed so sexual, so knowing, so sly and so strange. At once cocky and vulnerable. His face seemed full of sly understanding—a door to a world of unknown pleasures.

Some days later, my mother Sheila bought a copy of "Starman," just because she liked the song and Bowie's hair (she'd been a hairdresser in Liverpool before coming south and used to insist dogmatically that Bowie was wearing a wig from the late 1980s onward). I remember the slightly menacing black and white portrait photo of Bowie on the cover, shot from below, and the orange RCA Victor label on the seven-inch single.

For some reason, when I was alone with our tiny mono record player in what we called the dining room (though we didn't eat there—why would we?—there was no TV), I immediately flipped the single over to listen to the B side. I remember very clearly the physical reaction I felt listening to "Suffragette City." The sheer bodily excitement of that noise was almost too much to bear. I guess it sounded like . . . sex. Not that I knew what sex was. I was a virgin. I'd never even kissed anyone and had never wanted to. As Mick Ronson's guitar collided with my internal organs, I felt something strong and strange in my body that I'd never experienced before. Where was suffragette city? How did I get there?

I was twelve years old. My life had begun.

EPISODIC BLIPS

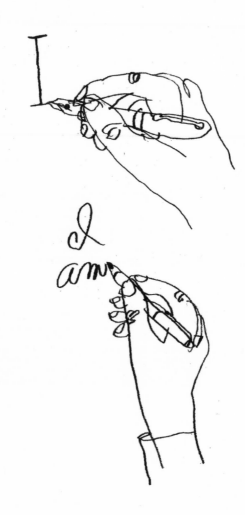

THERE IS A VIEW THAT SOME PEOPLE CALL "narrative identity." This is the idea that one's life is a kind of story, with a beginning, a middle, and an end. Usually there is some early, defining, traumatic experience and a crisis or crises in the middle (sex, drugs, any form of addiction will serve) from which one miraculously recovers. Such life stories usually culminate in redemption before ending with peace on earth and goodwill to all men. The unity of one's life consists in the coherence of the story one can tell about oneself. People do this all the time. It's the lie that stands behind the idea of the memoir. Such is the *raison d'être* of a big chunk of what remains of the publishing industry, which is fed by the ghastly gutter world of creative writing courses. Against this and with Simone Weil, I believe in *decreative* writing that moves through spirals of ever-ascending negations before reaching . . . nothing.

I also think that identity is a very fragile affair. It is at best a sequence of episodic blips rather than some grand narrative unity. As David Hume established long ago, our inner life is made up of disconnected bundles of perceptions that lie around like so much dirty laundry in the rooms of our memory. This is perhaps the reason why Brion Gysin's cut-up technique, where text is seemingly randomly spliced with scissors—and which Bowie famously borrowed from William Burroughs—gets so much closer to reality than any version of naturalism.

The episodes that give my life some structure are surprisingly often provided by David Bowie's words and music. He ties my life together like no one else I know. Sure, there are other memories and other stories that one might tell, and in my case this is complicated by the amnesia that followed a serious industrial accident when I was eighteen years old. I forgot a lot after my hand got stuck in a machine. But Bowie has been my sound track. My constant, clandestine companion. In good times and bad. Mine and his.

What's striking is that I don't think I am alone in this view. There is a world of people for whom Bowie was the being who permitted a powerful emotional connection and freed them to become some other kind of self, something freer, more queer, more honest, more open, and more exciting. Looking back, Bowie has become a kind of touchstone for that past, its glories and its glorious failures, but also for some kind of constancy in the present and for the possibility of a future, even the demand for a better future.

I don't mean this to sound hubristic. Look, I've never met the guy—Bowie, I mean—and I doubt

I ever will (and, to be honest, I don't really want to. I'd be terrified. What would I say? Thank you for the music? That's *so* ABBA). But I feel an extraordinary intimacy with Bowie, although I know this is a total fantasy. I also know that this is a shared fantasy, common to huge numbers of loyal fans for whom Bowie is not some rock star or a series of flat media clichés about bisexuality and bars in Berlin. He is someone who has made life a little less ordinary for an awfully long time.

THE ART'S
FILTHY LESSON

AFTER ANDY WARHOL HAD BEEN SHOT BY
Valerie Solanas in 1968, he said, "Before I was shot, I suspected that instead of living I'm just watching TV. Since being shot, I'm certain of it." Bowie's acute ten-word commentary on Warhol's statement, in the eponymous song from *Hunky Dory* in 1971, is deadly accurate: "Andy Warhol, silver screen / Can't tell them apart at all." The ironic self-awareness of the artist and their audience can only be that of their *inauthenticity*, repeated at increasingly conscious levels. Bowie repeatedly mobilizes this Warholian aesthetic.

The inability to distinguish Andy Warhol from the silver screen morphs into Bowie's continual sense of himself being stuck inside his own movie. Such is the conceit of "Life on Mars?," which begins with the "girl with the mousy hair," who is "hooked to the silver screen." But in the final verse, the movie's screenwriter is revealed as Bowie himself or his persona, although we can't tell them apart at all:

> But the film is a saddening bore
> 'Cause I wrote it ten times or more
> It's about to be writ again.

The conflation of life with a movie conspires with the trope of repetition to evoke a melancholic sense of being both bored and trapped. One becomes an actor in one's own movie. This is my sense of Bowie's much-misunderstood lines in "Quicksand":

> I'm living in a silent film
> Portraying Himmler's sacred realm
> Of dream reality.

Bowie displays an acute awareness of Himmler's understanding of National Socialism as political *artifice*, as an artistic and especially architectural construction, as well as a cinematic spectacle. Hitler, in the words of Hans-Jürgen Syberberg, was *ein Film aus Deutschland*, a film from Germany. As Bowie put it, Hitler was the first pop star. But being stuck inside a movie evokes not elation but depression and a Major Tom–like inaction:

> *I'm sinking in the quicksand of my thought*
> *And I ain't got the power anymore.*

In "Five Years," after having received the news that the Earth will soon die, Bowie sings, "And it was cold and it rained and I felt like an actor." Similarly, in one of my all-time favorite Bowie songs, "The Secret Life of Arabia" (outrageously and ferociously covered by the late, great Billy Mackenzie with the British Electric Foundation), Bowie sings,

You must see the movie
The sand in my eyes
I walk though a desert song
When the heroine dies.

The world is a film set, and the movie that's being shot might well be called *Melancholia*. One of Bowie's best and bleakest songs, "Candidate," begins with a statement of explicit pretense, "We'll pretend we're walking home," and is followed by the line, "My set is amazing, it even smells like a street."

Art's filthy lesson is inauthenticity all the way down, a series of repetitions and reenactments: fakes that strip away the illusion of reality in which we live and confront us with the reality of illusion. Bowie's world is like a dystopian version of *The Truman Show*, the sick place of the world that is forcefully expressed in the ruined, violent cityscapes of "Aladdin Sane" and "Diamond Dogs" and, more subtly, in the desolate soundscapes of

"Warszawa" and "Neuköln." To borrow Iggy Pop's idiom from *Lust for Life* (itself borrowed from Antonioni's 1975 movie, although Bowie might well be its implicit referent), Bowie is the passenger who rides through the city's ripped backside, under a bright and hollow sky.

WONDERFUL

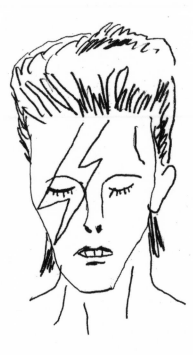

WHAT WAS THE SOURCE OF BOWIE'S POWER TO connect with ordinary boys and girls, maybe particularly the slightly alienated ones, the ones who felt bored and deeply awkward in their skin? The obvious answer is given in "Rock 'n' Roll Suicide," the final track on *Ziggy Stardust* and the song that Bowie used to close many of his shows. This is the song's climax:

> *Oh no love! You're not alone*
> *No matter what or who you've been*
> *No matter when or where you've seen*
> *All the knives seem to lacerate your brain*

I've had my share, I'll help you with the pain
You're not alone

Just turn on with me and you're not alone
Let's turn on with me and you're not alone
(wonderful)
Let's turn on and be not alone (wonderful)
Gimme your hands 'cause you're wonderful
(wonderful)
Gimme your hands 'cause you're wonderful
(wonderful)
Oh gimme your hands.

Bowie-as-Ziggy refused the dominant norms of existing society society: boy/girl, human/alien, gay/straight. He was the outsider, the alien, the visitor (the latter was the name that the humanoid alien Thomas Jerome Newton gave to his album—a message in a bottle back home—when Bowie played him in *The Man Who Fell to Earth* in 1976). Here was Ziggy in his suicide song reaching out to us in our dumb, tangled-up, self-lacerating suburban confusion and saying that we were wonderful. Millions of self-conscious mini-Hamlets living out their loveless hells in scattered, sundry hamlets, towns, and cities heard those words and were astonished at being forgiven. We just needed to reach out our hands. We did. We bought the album.

I AM A HEIDEGGERIAN BORE

IF BOWIE'S ART IS INAUTHENTIC, IF IT IS *F* FOR
Fake, as Orson Welles might have put it, then is it also
F for *Falsehood*? I remember reading an interview
many years ago with Robert Fripp where he talked
about watching Bowie in the studio in the late 1970s.
Bowie was listening to a track or a tape loop and was
very carefully, repeatedly, quite deliberately, and for
the longest time, trying to generate the right emotion
in his voice. What could be more contrived and fake
than that? Shouldn't true music come straight out of
the heart, up through the vocal cords, and into our
waiting, shell-like ears? Yet, as others have observed,
Bowie's genius lies in the meticulous matching of
mood with music through the medium of the voice.

If I were even more of a Heideggerian bore than I am, we could talk about the link between voice (*die Stimme*) and mood (*die Stimmung*) as that basic activity through which a world is disclosed to us, and disclosed, moreover, emotionally rather than rationally. Bowie's genius, then, is one of interpretation in the sense of *Auslegung*, or laying (*legen*) something out (*aus*), making it accord with us or resound for us sonorously in a way that can hit us hard or soft.

But we need to add an important caveat to this line of thought. Music like Bowie's is not a way of somehow recalling human beings affectively to a kind of pre-established harmony with the world. That would be banal and mundane, literally. Rather, Bowie permits a kind of *deworlding* of the world, an experience of mood, emotion, or *Stimmung* that shows that all in the world *stimmt nicht*—i.e., is not in agreement or accord with the self. In this sense, music is a discord with the world that can allow a certain demundanization, a withdrawal that might permit us to see things in a utopian light.

Anyone who has listened to Bowie over the years is completely familiar with the almost vaudeville or pantomime quality of his cast of stock characters. Each character has its distinctive voice: from the cheeky, mockney-cockney Tony Newley or even the bloody laughing gnome to the cherubic, mascara-daubed Anglo-surrealism of Syd Barrett to the dark, gravy-rich *basso profundo* of Scott Walker to a higher-pitched Iggy Pop (I am not the biggest fan of some of Bowie's Iggy imitations) to the breathy white soul-boy and on to the quasi-operatic or even hymnal, as on "Word on a Wing." Variations on these characters, and others, appear on album after album. We are not stupid. We know that they are all fakes.

So, how, in all this fakery, does something true emerge? One might reply that it just does, and you just feel it (or you don't—after all, there's no accounting for taste, particularly bad taste), citing that famous line from "Changes":

> *So I turned myself to face me*
> *But I've never caught a glimpse*
> *Of how the others must see the faker*
> *I'm much too fast to take that test.*

To turn yourself to face yourself is not to confront your authentic subjectivity. It is to see nothing, not even a glimpse. Warhol is the silver screen. Hang it on your wall. Nothing is hidden behind. Others may see this as fakery, but Bowie is too fast, as he arrogantly but rather accurately reports. He has already moved on to some new form.

Bowie's truth is inauthentic, completely self-conscious and utterly constructed. But it is still right, *es stimmt* as one can say in German, or it has the quality of feeling right, of being *stimmig*. We hear it and say "yes." Silently, or sometimes out loud. The sound of Bowie's voice creates a resonance within us. It finds a corporeal echo. But resonance invites dissonance. A resonating body in one location—like glasses on a table—begins to make another body shake and suddenly the whole floor is covered with broken glass. Music resounds and calls us to dissent from the world, to experience a *dissensus communis*, a sociability at odds with common sense. Through the fakery and because of it, we feel a truth that leads us beyond ourselves, toward the imagination of some other way of being.

Bowie's genius allows us to break the superficial link that seems to connect authenticity to truth. There is a truth to Bowie's art, a moodful truth, a heard truth, a felt truth, an embodied truth. Something heard with and within the body. The tone of the singing voice and music is felt in the *tonus* or musculature of the body. Musical tension is muscular, rising or falling, in progressive wave-beats of pleasure.

UTOPIAN SOMETHING

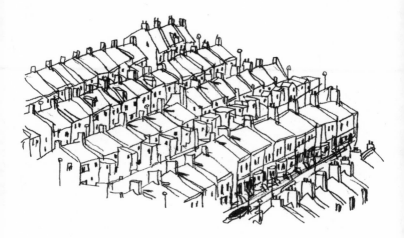

BOWIE INCARNATED A UTOPIAN SOMETHING: some other way of existing in the suburban shitholes of Bromley, Beckenham, Billericay, Basingstoke, Braintree, or Biggleswade. It wasn't some reflection of life on the street. Why would we have been interested in that? Life was routine, gray, cramped, and dull. Our parents were deeply morally confused by the 1960s, having affairs, getting divorced, and wearing flared trousers. We were just bored. BORED. Let the upper-middle classes celebrate street life after their winter skiing trips with their parents or taking the Volvo on a tour of the Dordogne. Bowie represented something else, especially for intelligently disaffected ordinary boys and girls. It was something impossibly glamorous and strange. It rejected the street.

As Jon Savage rightly puts it, Bowie was not about any sort of realism. His success connected with a latent, low-budget science-fiction exuberance (more Michael Moorcock than Isaac Asimov; more *Quatermass and the Pit* than *Star Trek*) that was a template for the ruined landscapes through which the spaceboys and girls of glam, punk, and post-punk would run wearing outrageous, often homemade and slightly crappy outfits. It was what Nicholas Pegg calls, in a choice phrase, a "Home Counties apocalypse," complete with milk floats and the mental hospitals that encircled London at the time. As others have pointed out, Bowie spoke to the weirdos and the freaks. But it turned out that there were a lot of us. It left you wondering: who exactly were the insiders? Much, much later, Bowie found a new word to name them: *heathen*. We simply didn't want to be heathen.

A SEER
IS A LIAR

CONSIDER BOWIE'S LYRICS. IT SEEMS THAT WE simply cannot help but read them autobiographically, as clues and signs that would lead us to some authentic sense of the "real" Bowie, his past, his traumas, his loves, his political views. We long to see his songs as windows onto his life. But this is precisely what we have to give up if we want to try and misunderstand Bowie a little less. As we know all too well, he occupies and has always occupied a variety of identities. His brilliance is to become someone else for the length of a song, sometimes for a whole album or even a tour. Bowie is a ventriloquist.

This wasn't a strategy that died with Ziggy onstage at the Hammersmith Odeon in 1973. It persists right through to Bowie's most recent album, *The Next Day*, where many of the songs are written from an other's identity, whether the menacing and dumb perpetrator of a mass shooting, as on "Valentine's Day," or the enigmatic persona on the album's final track, "Heat." The latter has perhaps the strongest and most oblique lyric on the album, which concerns a son's loathing for a father who either ran a prison or turned their home into a prison. There is an apparent allusion to Mishima's *Spring Snow* and the following arresting image:

Then we saw Mishima's dog
Trapped between the rocks
Blocking the waterfall.

Bowie sings repeatedly, "And I tell myself, I don't know who I am." The song ends with the line, "I am a seer, I am a liar." To which we might add, Bowie is a seer *because* he is a liar. The truth content of Bowie's art is not compromised by its fakery. It is enabled by it.

Otherwise said, Bowie evokes truth through "Oblique Strategies," which was the name given to a series of more than a hundred cards that Brian Eno created with artist Peter Schmidt in 1975. For example, during the recording of "V-2 Schneider" (the title is both a pun on the V-2 rocket that decimated parts of London in 1944 and the two core members of Kraftwerk—*we two* = Ralf Hütter and Florian Schneider), Bowie accidentally began playing the sax on the offbeat. Just prior to the recording, he had read one of the "Oblique Strategies" cards, which read, "Honor thy errors for their hidden intentions." Thus the track was born. I would insist that Bowie's lyrics demand to be understood in relation to a similar discipline of the oblique.

In my humble opinion, authenticity is the curse of music from which we need to cure ourselves.

Bowie can help. His art is a radically contrived and reflexively aware confection of illusion whose fakery is not false, but at the service of a felt, corporeal truth. As he sings in "Quicksand,"

> *Don't believe in yourself*
> *Don't deceive with belief.*

To push this a little further, perhaps music at its most theatrical, extravagant, and absurd is also the truest music. It is what can save us from ourselves, from the banal fact of being in the world. Such music, Bowie's music, can allow us to escape from being riveted to the fact of who we are, to escape from being us. For a moment, we can be lifted up, elevated, and turned around. At their very highest level, songs can, with words, rhythm, and often simple, nursery-rhyme melodies, begin to connect up the dots of what we think of as a life. Episodic blips. They can also allow us to think of another life.

As fragile and inauthentic as our identities are, Bowie let us (and still lets us) believe that we can reinvent ourselves. In fact, we can reinvent ourselves *because* our identities are so fragile and inauthentic. Just as Bowie seemingly reinvented himself without limits, he allowed us to believe that our own capacity for changes was limitless. Of course, there are limits—profound limits, mortal limits—in reshaping who we are. But somehow, in listening to his songs—even now—one hears an extraordinary hope that we are not alone and this place can be escaped, just for a day.

HOLD ON
TO NOTHING

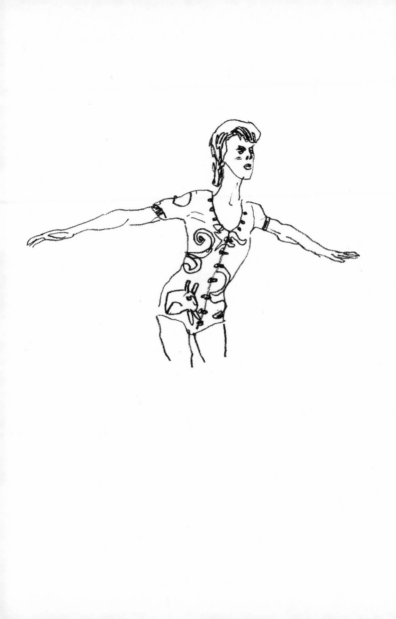

BACK THEN, WHEN I WAS TWELVE YEARS OLD, although I couldn't have put any of it into words (I didn't have many words; my family rarely talked about anything apart from football, TV, and the contents of the emergently hegemonic *Sun* newspaper and the evergreen-until-it-was-killed *News of the World*), Bowie showed us another way of being a boy or a girl or something else entirely. Bowie-as-Ziggy recalibrated sexuality in a way that was debauched but distilled, decidedly racy but also refined. It was a kind of degenerate asceticism. Whatever sexuality was on display, it was not the kind of hairy 1960s variety that our parents were becoming accustomed to through grainy, badly lit sex scenes in the movies or the terrifyingly hirsute illustrations in Alex Comfort's *The Joy of Sex*. This was a kind of alien sex, literally like the sex scene in *The Man Who Fell to Earth* where Bowie as Thomas Jerome Newton removes his eyelids, nipples, and genitals before showing his true, alien form to his girlfriend Mary-Lou. She is completely horrified. They both decide to get drunk.

Alienation was confronted through a confrontation with the alien. For me, it was learning how to come into an already alienated sexuality by loving the alien. When we eventually worked our way back through Bowie's pre-Ziggy catalogue, we learned to call such states "ch-ch-ch-ch-changes," where "we turn and face the strange." What can I say? It made sense like nothing else I'd experienced. True, this whole trope of androgyny and floating boy/girl identities became completely vulgarized in the horrors of British glam rock, with bands like the Sweet, Gary Glitter, and the execrable Mud. By the time Bowie's "Rebel, Rebel" was released early in 1974 with the line, "You've got your mother in a whirl / Coz she's not sure that you're a boy or a girl," it was clear that the game was up. Todd Haynes's lovingly evocative film *Velvet Goldmine* (1998) gets the mood of these years absolutely right.

Bowie's bold act of creative/destructive genius was very simple: having got millions of kids like me to believe in the illusion of Ziggy as some Nietzschean *Übermensch* figure, he destroyed him. He killed Ziggy onstage at the Hammersmith Odeon on July 3, 1973, three days short of the anniversary of his 1972 appearance on *Top of the Pops*. Ziggy had lasted barely a year. Having created the illusion of the superman, he then popped it like a balloon.

Of course, had we not been kids or if we'd been as clever as Bowie at the time, we could have seen this coming. *The Man Who Sold the World*—an important and misunderstood album in my view—ends with a track called "The Supermen." Bowie asks, who are the Nietzschean supermen, these creatures that have left behind the human condition? Far from paradise and way to the east of Eden, they lead

> *Tragic endless lives*
> *Could heave nor sigh in solemn perverse serenity*
> *Wondrous beings chained to life.*

The more-than-human, infinite life of the superman is a cruel torture. All he craves is a chance to die.

Here we begin to see a productive tension in Bowie's work. On the one hand, the fantasy of the superman is a tragic disaster that craves only what he can't have: death. Therefore, Ziggy's suicide is a kind of release from that fantasy after having traversed it experientially. On the other hand, as Bowie writes in "After All," also from *The Man Who Sold the World*, "Man is an obstacle, sad as the clown (oh by jingo)."

The overcoming of the human condition is a disaster, yet man is still an obstacle. We're human, all-too-human, and yet long to overcome that condition. Much of Bowie's work circles obsessively around this dilemma.

How does one live with and within this tension and the restlessness and disquiet that it induces? The next line of "After All" is revealing: "So hold on to nothing, and he won't let you down (oh by jingo)." I want to hold on to this figure of nothing as I think it gives us a clue for understanding a persistent feature of Bowie's work. The word *nothing* keeps recurring in his words and the affects that those words seek to mark. For example, in "'Heroes,'" Bowie sings, "We're nothing and nothing can help us."

At the core of Bowie's music is the exhilaration of an experience of nothing and the attempt to hold on to it. This doesn't mean that Bowie is a nihilist. Au contraire.

HAMLET
IN
SPACE

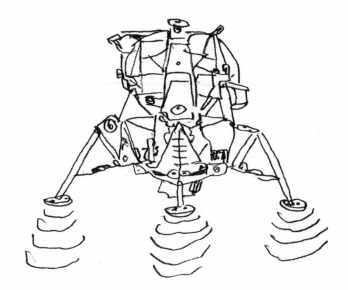

CONSIDER BOWIE'S UNDERRATED, FIRST 1969
hit, "Space Oddity" (or odd ditty—it is a fascinating conjecture, following Nicholas Pegg, to ponder the possibility that Major Tom was Tom Major, the father of former British Prime Minister John Major, whose name would have appeared on various variety bills in Brixton, where young David Jones, later Bowie, was born). Major Tom goes into space and becomes a media commodity. ("The papers want to know whose shirts you wear.") But rather than being overjoyed at having exceeded the terrestrial limit of the human condition, Major Tom withdraws into melancholic inaction.

The epic political comedy of the Apollo 11 moon landing in July 1969 becomes a one-act tragic farce called *Hamlet in Space*. Yet unlike the melancholy Dane, Major Tom's suicidal desire is not underwritten by an appeal to any transcendent deity. Hamlet's first lines onstage are "That the Everlasting had not fixed his canon 'gainst self-slaughter" (Bowie assumed the persona of Hamlet to great effect, holding Yorick's skull when he sang "Cracked Actor" during the *David Live* tour in 1974). Against this, Major Tom passively intones,

> *I'm feeling very still*
> *And I think my spaceship knows which way to go*
> *Tell my wife I love her very much*
> *She knows.*

Going into space leads to a successful suicide attempt, which leaves Major Tom finally inert, holding on to nothing.

> *Planet Earth is blue*
> *And there's nothing I can do.*

In a beautifully reflexive gesture, "Ashes to Ashes" from 1980 provides a perspicuous commentary on this moment in "Space Oddity":

> *Ashes to ashes, funk to funky*
> *We know Major Tom's a junky*
> *Strung out in heavens high*
> *Hitting an all-time low.*

Of course, these words are self-referential, where the "all-time low" is both the title of Bowie's 1977 album, *Low*, and the experience that album tries to evoke and escape: depression caused by drug addiction. It would appear that Major Tom had been popping more than protein pills.

The flipside of the blissful inaction of "Space Oddity" is the messianic promise of "Starman," waiting in the sky. Although he'd like to come and meet us, the song continues, the Starman thinks he'd blow our minds. So, we don't have direct contact with the Starman. We just hear about him from his prophet, Ziggy. The point is that the Messiah doesn't come and anything that has the redemptive patina of a God-man, whether Ziggy or Major Tom or indeed Bowie himself, has to die.

DYSTOPIA— GET IT HERE, THING

ONE OF THE STRANGEST MOMENTS IN THE
history of British popular music is Peter Noone's
cover version of "Oh! You Pretty Things," which
did pretty well on the UK charts in 1971. Noone
(whose name wonderfully splits open into "no
one"—a little like Odysseus's reply to the Cyclops
Polyphemus) had been the frontman of the oddly
named but hugely successful Herman's Hermits.
Noone displayed a truly bravura lack of understanding of Bowie's lyrics, which are replete with
references to Nietzsche's *Zarathustra*. More precisely, the song asserts the uselessness of *homo
sapiens* and the need to make way for the *homo
superior*. Admittedly, this is all framed in a rather

cheap, British, BBC, *Doctor Who* version of the future. But the point is clear enough: the extraterrestrial strangers have come to take our children toward a nonhuman future. For us, the nightmare has begun and "We've finished our news."

Funniest of all, fearful of radio censorship, Noone replaced Bowie's "the earth is a bitch" with the apparently more upbeat "the earth is a beast" (but a bitch is a beast, you might quip). The basis, the constant, the ground of Bowie's most important work is that the world is screwed, used up, old and done. The earth is a dying dog that awaits its beating from a new master. Bowie's vision is continually dystopian. One can hear this in the pre-apocalyptic melancholy of "Five Years," or indeed in post-apocalyptic visions like "Drive-In Saturday." In the latter, the survivors of a nuclear catastrophe live in vast domes in the western desert of the USA using old movies in order to reenact what they imagine ordinary life was like before the war, "Like the video films we saw." But, of course, what is created in this reen-actment is not the past, but the clichéd schlock of 1950s romantic movies, where "His name was always Buddy."

But the most profound and extended dystopian vision comes after the introduction of Gysin's cut-up method in *Diamond Dogs* in April 1974, what Peter Doggett calls Bowie's "dark study in cultural disintegration." Whatever judgments we might make about Bowie's musical development, *Diamond Dogs* is a courageous conceptual step into new territory. To my mind, it is the album where Bowie finally rids himself of the ghost of Ziggy and begins the rich and speedy series of aesthetic transformations that will carry through until *Scary Monsters* in 1980. Despite its obvious, repeated acts of homage to the Rolling Stones, particularly through Bowie's wonderfully scratchy and slightly twisted Keith Richards guitar imita-tions, the album pushes past whatever rock 'n' roll had been, slashing and mutilating it before carting it off to the graveyard: "This ain't rock 'n' roll. This is genocide."

I remember looking at the cover of the album, where Bowie is stretched out, half-Great Dane, half-human, for what seemed like hours in the window of our local record store. Then, inside the listening booth (such places still existed at the time), I heard the opening track, "Future Legend," where the howls of wolves ran alongside the tune from "Bewitched, Bothered and Bewildered," which I knew from one of my mother's Sinatra albums.

Inspired by Burroughs's *Wild Boys*, with marauding gangs carrying eighteen-inch bowie knives that cut two ways, a premonition of the suburban boys and girls who would hit the streets of sundry decaying British cities in the riotous days of punk, *Diamond Dogs* begins with the prophecy of "Future Legend." Bowie's words also cut two ways:

And in the death
As the last few corpses lay rotting on the slimy thoroughfare
The shutters lifted in inches in temperance building
High on Poacher's Hill
And red mutant eyes gaze down on Hunger City
No more big wheels

Fleas the size of rats sucked on rats the size of cats
And ten thousand peoploids split into small tribes
Coveting the highest of the sterile skyscrapers
Like packs of dogs assaulting the glass fronts of Love-Me Avenue
Ripping and rewrapping mink and shiny silver fox, now legwarmers
Family badge of sapphire and cracked emerald
Any day now the year of the diamond dogs.

Bowie has a vision of the world as ruined: complete civilizational collapse. Here is a picture of urban space prior to gentrification (bliss it was to be alive in that twilight), a space of crime and inverted consumerism. Tramps wear diamonds, silver fox fur becomes legwarmers, heraldic emblems of jewels become rich trash to be draped around freakish peoploids.

LES
TRICOTEUSES

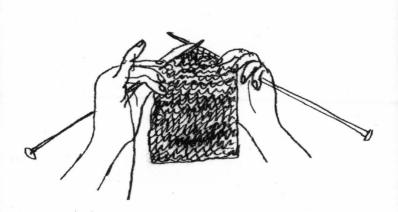

BOWIE'S ALBUMS OFTEN HAVE TRACES OF

musical styles that are being abandoned, like out-
worn skins, alongside the premonition of something
new that will find voice in future work. In *Diamond
Dogs*, the songs "Rebel, Rebel" and "Rock 'n' Roll
with Me" belong to that past, and arguably the
soulful, Isaac Hayes–influenced wah-wah guitar of
"1984" points forward toward *Young Americans*.
But the real innovations are the nine-minute
sequence of "Sweet Thing," "Candidate," and
"Sweet Thing (Reprise)" and the nightmarishly brilliant "We Are the Dead" (and we could also make
a good case for "Chant of the Ever Circling Skeletal
Family"; on the original vinyl version of *Diamond*

Dogs that I owned in the 1970s, the needle would get stuck at the end of the track, emitting an endless and increasingly disturbing "bro, bro, bro, bro, bro, bro, bro, bro, bro, bro").

In the dead diamond dog world of Halloween Jack (one of the personae on the album), sex is no longer some transgressive excitement. It is "putting pain in a stranger." Its image, like a Bacon painting, is "a portrait in flesh, who trails on a leash." If this is a world of flesh, then that flesh is dying. We find here an almost paranoid-schizophrenic picture of the world as extinct, rotting and in need of redemption. This is the kind of world that we find in President Schreber's deliciously strange delusions in *Memoirs of My Nervous Illness*, or the inhabitants of R. D. Laing's Kingsley Hall free asylum in London in the late 1960s: "Can't you tell I'm dead? I can smell the flesh rotting."

Perhaps there is also some memory of the world of Bowie's schizophrenic half brother, Terry Burns, from whom he learned so much so early (about jazz, about Jack Kerouac, about wandering around seedy Soho in London), and who, after he had been institutionalized in a mental hospital for many years, somehow thought that David could save him. Terry Burns killed himself in the final days of 1984 at Coulsdon South railway station, south of London, by putting his head on the rails and waiting for the train to approach. Bowie set off a family feud and media storm by not attending the funeral. He didn't want to turn it into a circus. The note on Bowie's bouquet was extremely poignant: "You've seen more things than we can imagine, but all these moments will be lost—like tears washed away by the rain."

It has often been said that there is something of the psychotic in Bowie, which I rather doubt. Bowie was not a lad insane. If such psychotic tendencies exist, then—as with Joyce in *Finnegans Wake* or as with Artaud in his Theatre of Cruelty—they are sublimated into art. Thanks to his art, maybe he's not crazy, or so crazy. The constant references to madness, paranoia, and delusion, particularly in the early tracks on *The Man Who Sold the World*, are a musical transformation of its terrors, even the crazy, closing, canine chant to "All the Madmen": "Zane, zane, zane. *Ouvrez le chien.*"

That said, a mad, dead half-brother is a kind of shadow figure and a history of madness in a family, as seems to have been the case with Bowie's mother, Margaret Mary Burns, is a terrifying thing. We are the dead. The air is full of their cries.

"Is it nice in your snow storm, freezing your brain?" Bowie asks. It's the exhilarating bleakness of Bowie's vision in *Diamond Dogs* that pulls me in with its dirty claws. As the protagonist in the track "Candidate" walks through his film set that "even smells like a street," he boasts,

> *Someone scrawled on the wall, 'I smell the*
> *blood of* les tricoteuses'
> *Who wrote up scandals in other bars.*

The *tricoteuses* were the insurrectionary, working-class Parisian women who cheered on executions during the Terror of 1793 to 1794 while watching the surgically precise work of Madame Guillotine. "Candidate" builds with a terrifying lyrical force, painting the picture of a world of exploitation, decay, and rape:

> *Till the sun beats love on the seedy young knights*
> *Who press you on the ground while shaking in fright.*

The world is a prostituted sexual hell defined by random ultra-violence. The song ends plaintively and desperately:

> *I guess we could cruise down one more time*
> *With you by my side it should be fine*

We'll buy some drugs and watch a band
Then jump in the river holding hands.

The only possible connection in a desperate, ruined world, the sole remainder of love, is to take some drugs and carry out a suicide pact, like the German writer Heinrich von Kleist and Henriette Vogel, who killed themselves on the shore of the Wannsee outside Berlin after drinking coffee they had brought to them from a nearby café. In a loveless world, love can only be saved through death.

THE MAJESTY
OF THE ABSURD

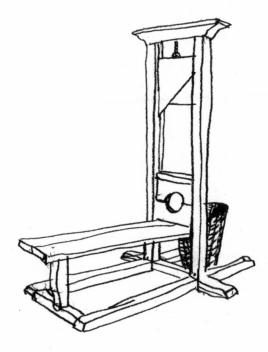

I WANT TO GO BACK TO THE ALLUSION TO *les tricoteuses* and make a little leap here, or at least take a small step. When I listen to *Diamond Dogs* and think about Bowie's dystopian vision, I think of Georg Büchner's *Danton's Death* (*Dantons Tod*). This extraordinary play is defined by a post-revolutionary sense of despair, inaction, and pervasive nihilism. Just prior to his execution, the imprisoned Danton says,

> Everything is packed and swarming. The nothing has killed itself (*das Nichts hat sich ermordert*). Creation is its wound. We are its drops of blood, and the world the grave in which it rots.

Such, I think, is Bowie's dystopia defined by Enlightenment's deadly dialectic. We declare that God is dead and turn ourselves into Gods only in order to kill better, to exterminate more effectively. We have become heathen. Danton goes on,

> The world is chaos. Nothingness is the world-god waiting yet to be born (*das Nichts ist das zu gebärende Weltgott*).

Danton's Death ends with Lucile—most Ophelia-like—mounting the steps of the guillotine where the guards are sleeping. She shouts, "Long live the King! (*Es lebe der König!*)" It seems like a suicidal gesture and one imagines that she is swiftly dispatched, although Büchner leaves the audience to draw that inference. Yet, Paul Celan, in his justly famous "Meridian" speech, given when accepting the Büchner Prize in 1960, finds another meaning to Lucile's words. He insists that "It is an act of freedom. It is a step." If that step might appear to be a reactionary defense of the *ancien régime,* then Celan counters,

> But it is not. Allow me, who grew up on the writings of Peter Kropotkin and Gustav Landauer, to insist: this is not homage to any monarchy, to any yesterday worth preserving.

> It is homage to the majesty of the absurd which bespeaks the presence of human beings.

> This, Ladies and Gentlemen, has no definitive name, but I believe that this is . . . poetry (*die Dichtung*).

Fascinatingly, Celan places Lucile's act under the aegis of Kropotkin's anarchism of mutual aid and Landauer's more heady mystical anarchism. Slightly further on, Celan adds what he calls a "topological" dimension to this thought. To take Lucile's step is to see things "in a u-topian light." Therefore, the act of freedom which is poetry is u-topian:

We came into the nearness of the open and the free. And finally into the nearness of Utopia.

Poetry is a step, an act of freedom taken in relation to a world defined by the majesty of the absurd, a human world. Thus, Büchner's dystopia is the condition for utopia. My only real thought about Bowie is that his art is also such a step. It sets us free in relation to a civilization that is petrified and dead. One does not fix up a house that is falling off a cliff. Bowie's dystopia is utopian in equal measure.

I think this thought casts a different light on Bowie's vision of the world and world politics. Consider a track like the stunning "It's No Game," which appears in two versions ("Part 1" and "Part 2") as bookends to *Scary Monsters*. Tony Visconti revealed that, amazingly, both versions have the same backing track, although at that point the similarities end. Where the second version is flat, direct, and affectless, the first version features Bowie at his most powerfully histrionic, accompanied by a menacing voiceover in Japanese by Michi Hirota and an insane guitar part by Robert Fripp. The track finishes with Bowie screaming "shut up" over Fripp's seemingly endless, repeating guitar riff.

What Bowie describes is a Büchnerian world of terror. The first line, "Silhouettes and shadows watch the revolution," describes the languor and disappointment of a post-revolutionary situation. In an allusion to Eddie Cochran's posthumously released 1960 hit, there are no longer "three steps to heaven." All that remains are "Big heads and drums—full speed and pagan." "So, where's the moral?" Bowie asks. "People have their fingers broken." In the final verse of "Part 2," Bowie concludes,

> *Children round the world*
> *Put camel shit on the walls*

> *They're making carpets on treadmills*
> *Or garbage sorting.*

So, where's the moral in all this camel shit? Pop stars, like the dreadful Bono, are meant to morph into slimmer versions of Salman Rushdie and mouth liberal platitudes about the state of the world and what we can do to put it right. But here Bowie gives the lie to such liberal complacency by exposing it to a simple, visceral critique. The inexpensive carpets that we use to furnish our home are made by those living in camel-shit huts. Rather than amuse ourselves by playing with some fraudulent political agenda, Bowie simply declares that "It's no game." Shit is serious.

The next track on *Scary Monsters*, "Up the Hill Backwards," begins, "The vacuum created by the arrival of freedom, and the possibilities it seems to offer." Like Lucile's cry at the end of *Danton's Death*, this line sounds like Edmund Burke's conservative critique of the French Revolution. But adapting Celan's logic, this is no homage to any monarchy or any yesterday, apart from the majesty of the absurd, which is the world of human beings. Such is poetry in Celan's sense, Bowie's poetry.

ILLUSION
TO
ILLUSION

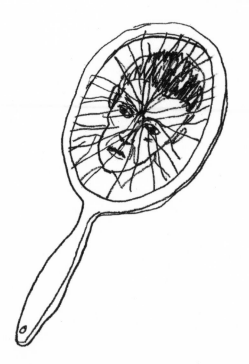

WE WERE YOUNG AND DUMB BACK THEN AT
twelve, thirteen, and fourteen years old. But
Bowie taught us both the deceptive nature of illusion and its irresistible power. We learned to live
with illusion and learn from illusion rather than
run away from it. To inhabit this space is also to
live *after* the revolution, in the *dis*-illusion that
follows a revolutionary sequence. For us, this was
the fucked-up, disappointed solidarity of the early
1970s most powerfully expressed in "All the Young
Dudes," written by Bowie for Mott the Hoople.
This song was like Kerouac's *On the Road* for a
beaten generation who knew they were going absolutely nowhere:

*My brother's back at home with his Beatles
and his Stones
We never got it off on that revolution stuff
. . . What a drag . . . too many snags.*

We followed Bowie from illusion to illusion. As he gradually ceased to be the huge mainstream pop star that he was in the Ziggy period, my interest in him only intensified.

In February 1976, I stole a secondhand copy of *Station to Station* from David's (no relation) Bookshop in Letchworth Garden City. I was nearly sixteen and felt that something was beginning to change in both Bowie and myself. The ten-minute and fourteen-second title track (Bowie's longest) seemed to open a door onto a new landscape of musical possibilities. Importantly, whatever this was didn't have a name. But it was no longer rock and roll. That's why I liked it.

Like so many of my generation, by this time I was listening to a weird cocktail that included Detroit rock and roll, like Iggy and the Stooges and the mighty MC5, combined with the proto-ambient sound spaces of Terry Riley and Fripp & Eno. At the same time, I was particularly obsessed with the flood of new music coming out of the erstwhile West Germany, especially bands like Neu!, Can, Tangerine Dream, Popul Vuh, Amon Düül II, as well as the strangely monumental French band, Magma.

I remember walking into John Menzies newsagents in Letchworth late one afternoon in January 1977 and listening to *Low* with the girl who worked there, whom I fancied rather a lot without ever telling her. We listened to the whole album at the back of the shop. Although it sounded like it was recorded in outer space and we'd never heard drums sound quite like that and so far up in the mix, it made perfect sense to us. Even the ambient and instrumental side two. It was a cold winter and this was the chilliest modernism. I was ready for it. For reasons that I still don't understand, I spent four months at the end of 1976 in complete solitude, apart from forced interactions with my mother and odd days and Saturday mornings working in a sheet-metal factory with my dad. So, when Bowie half sang the words, in "Sound and Vision," "Drifting into my solitude," it had a profound effect. I too had been low.

Punk changed all that, and by March 1977 I was wearing black bondage trousers, a Lewis leather jacket, and twelve-hole Dr. Martens boots. I'd been playing off and on in crappy bands for a couple of years with names like the Social Class Five and Panik (with a k, just to be Germanic). When *Heroes* was released just ten months after *Low*, in October 1977, it hit those of us who heard it with extraordinary force. Not so much the title track, which I now like much more than I did back then, but the thick, rich, layered, complex density of the production in tracks like "Beauty and the Beast" and especially "Blackout." It also sounded black and was as funky as hell, driven on by Bowie's best rhythm section of Dennis Davis, Georges Murray, and Carlos Alomar. Robert Fripp's Frippertronics floated above in the ether. I wore out two copies of *"Heroes"* by imitating the bass parts on my Fender Jazz copy, and lost my third. I thought to myself and told anyone whose ear I could bend that *this* was how music should sound. I still think that's true. The effects of the recording and production techniques in *"Heroes"* can still be heard loud and clear in contemporary music—for example the Arcade Fire's stunning *Reflektor* from 2013, which features a one-word cameo from Bowie.

The huge anticipation surrounding *Lodger* in May 1979 meant that the album had to be a disappointment with too many obsessively reworked, repetitive loops turned into songs and an oddly thin sound. Some of those loops worked, like "Red Sails," a worthy homage to Neu! "Repetition" is a song of great power about domestic violence that works because of its lack of direct moralizing, delivered by Bowie in an affectless monotone. I remember sitting alone cross-legged on the floor of my mum's flat gazing at the distorted accident-victim image of Bowie on the cover and trying to like the album more and find ways of forgiving slightly dumb tracks like "Yassassin," the dreaded white reggae cover (for Bowie to sound even remotely like Sting was unbearable).

Scary Monsters was a different story. By this time, after an embarrassing two-year spell at a local catering college (my school had closed and been turned into an unemployment-benefit office and the college was just next door—call me lazy) and having failed to become a rock star, I was on the dole and went to do some courses at Stevenage Further Education College (let's just say that it wasn't exactly Harvard). I didn't have the money to buy albums, so I listened to a friend's copy at the student union during lunchtimes. I was overwhelmed by the self-reflexive brilliance of "Ashes to Ashes" and "Teenage Wildlife." Bowie looked at himself, knowing that everyone was looking at him. But I remember having the distinct feeling of a door being closed. *Scary Monsters* was acutely self-conscious of the instrumental role that Bowie had played at every stage in the development of punk and post-punk. It was kind of a meta-album. But there was something sad about it. Or maybe that sadness was mine. I had begun to discover another world of pleasure in words and was writing truly awful poetry. A year or so later, I went to university and things changed. I learned to pretend I didn't love Bowie as much as I did.

DISCIPLINE

IN HIS BOOK *THE MAN WHO SOLD THE WORLD:*
David Bowie and the 1970s, Peter Doggett argues
that Bowie was an anachronism in the upbeat,
libertarian world of the 1960s, but by the 1970s
his audience had caught up with him and his
picture of a world defined by fragmentation,
decay, and disappointment. Having killed Ziggy,
Bowie moved relentlessly from illusion to illusion, following an artistic pattern of inhabitation,
imitation, perfection, and destruction. It's a little
like Gustav Metzger's idea of auto-destructive
art, and Bowie is perhaps a more persuasive
example than Metzger's erstwhile student Pete
Townshend, when the Who used to auto-destruc-

tively smash up all their equipment at the end of a show. This fourfold pattern is perhaps clearest in the inhabitation of American soul and R & B in *Young Americans*. A perfect imitation of a genre also leads to its subtle elevation and then Bowie gets bored, destroys it, and moves on. *Station to Station* is informed by clear traces of *Young Americans*, but is already shedding its skin and looking forward to *Low*.

The point is that during the 1970s, especially from 1974 onward, Bowie was able to mobilize an artistic *discipline* that is terrifying in its intensity, daring, and risk. It is the very opposite of rock-star complacency. It is as if Bowie, almost ascetically, almost eremitically, disciplined himself into becoming a nothing, a mobile and massively creative nothing that could assume new faces, generate new illusions, and create new forms. This is weird and rare. Perhaps it is unique in the history of popular music.

After having made thirteen solo albums between 1969 and 1980, excluding live recordings, compilations, plus all that he did for Lou Reed on *Transformer* (Reed's best-selling and best solo album), for Iggy Pop on the monumental *The Idiot* and *Lust for Life*, for Mott the Hoople, and even for plucky little Lulu, Bowie effectively disappears in 1980. As Doggett insists, Bowie reappears in 1983 as the kind of blond, suntanned, smooth, chatty entertainer he had so fiercely ridiculed in the 1970s. I remember going to see him at the Milton Keynes Bowl in July 1983 when his band included Carlos Alomar and Earl Slick. Tickets cost a fortune and I felt absolutely flat throughout. I just remember being annoyed because I lost my glasses and couldn't read the copy of Heidegger's *Being and Time* that I had brought along with me. That's about it.

We mustn't forget that there have been awful moments to be a Bowie fan. There have been some illusions I really could have done without. Not so much *Let's Dance* (1983), which has several fine moments (I had been an assiduous student in producer Nile Rodgers's school of funk for many years), but the slow and seemingly irreversible decline that was palpable on *Tonight* (1984), apart from "Loving the Alien," and the truly execrable *Never Let Me Down* (1987). Bowie had somehow become convinced that covering and killing songs that he had co-written with Iggy, like "Neighborhood Threat," was a good idea. It was really horrible and heartbreaking.

But wait, things got even worse. Bowie had the terrific idea of forming an honest, go-ahead rock band called Tin Machine with a HUGE drum sound. Now, there are some good moments on the two Tin Machine albums, like the wonderful pastiche of Warholian indifference "I Can't Read," which has the great line, "Money goes to money heaven / Bodies go to body hell." But does one track redeem the tub-thumping, macho rockiness of Tin Machine? No way.

DISAPPEARANCE

THE 1990S WERE A DIFFERENT STORY. EACH OF
the four solo albums Bowie released during that decade had its specific virtues, as well as one or two vices. I couldn't make up my mind about *Black Tie/ White Noise* (1993), although I listened to it a lot, and loved the happy, clappy abandon of the newly married Bowie on tracks like "Miracle Goodnight" and "Don't Let Me Down and Down." I was living in Frankfurt when *Earthling* was released in 1997 and was (I am ashamed to admit) still trying to go out clubbing during the heyday of the introduction of London drum and bass into Germany, though I could never figure out how to dance to it. I therefore had serious qualms about the drum and

bass experiments of *Earthling*, despite loving the harmonic complexity of tracks like "Looking for Satellites." The heavily retrospective and slightly claustrophobic *Hours . . .* from 1999, which was widely marketed as a kind of *Summa* of Bowie's work that claimed to revisit each key moment in his development (it didn't), was a disappointment for me, although "Survive" and "Thursday's Child" are really quite wonderful songs.

But then I remember listening to *1.Outside* over and over and over again on a tiny cassette player in my girlfriend's kitchen in Stockholm in the winter of 1995 and smiling to myself saying, "Yes, this is it. This is it." I danced my legs down to the knees in that kitchen during those weeks, miming songs like a total fool, especially "No Control" and "The Motel."

Some years passed. Then, in June 2002, I was absolutely astonished and delighted at the appearance of *Heathen*, whose title track alone is breathtaking in its musical directness, subtlety, and economy. Here was a different Bowie: reflective, deep, somber, but still witty. The media declared it a post-9/11 Bowie. I was more skeptical. Heathen was quickly followed by *Reality* in 2003. These albums form a kind of pair, released in speedy succession, to the detriment of *Reality*, a really underrated album and the better of the two in my opinion. I remember driving around the Essex countryside in my Vauxhall Corsa listening to "New Killer Star" and "She'll Drive the Big Car." Bowie had also rediscovered the art of the ballad in this period on tracks like "Sunday," "5:15 The Angels Have Gone," and "The Loneliest Guy." A sublimely healthy-looking Bowie, with amazing, lovely white teeth—a real tribute to his New York orthodontist—kept appearing on British talk shows and seemed completely in control, expertly deflecting unwelcome questions with wit. . . .

. . . And then nothing. Radio silence. I moved to New York City, Bowie's adopted home. Maybe I would bump into him in the street. In 2004, there were stories of a heart attack in Germany, followed by rumors of illness, of lung cancer, of emphysema, all sorts of maladies. Late one night in Manhattan a few years back, I found myself in the apartment directly beneath Bowie's while visiting a friend. I kept looking at the ceiling nervously, feeling like a sad middle-aged stalker. I even forced the host to play the whole of *Ziggy Stardust*, although very quietly, just in case he was trying to sleep. I had the weirdest dreams when I got home to bed.

YEARNING

BOWIE'S MUSIC IS VERY OFTEN VIEWED AS isolated, withdrawn, solipsistic, and even autistic (as if we knew what that meant). This is a view that can be found in Hugo Wilcken's fine little book on *Low* and which is most obviously expressed in "Sound and Vision," with another couple of nothings:

> *Pale blinds drawn all day*
> *Nothing to do, nothing to say.*

This electric blue mood is continued in the perfectly entitled "Always Crashing in the Same Car." The latter apparently relates to an actual accident where Bowie smashed his Mercedes in a hotel garage in Switzerland. But it is more powerful as a metaphor for addictive, destructive loops of behavior.

I am not saying that this view is wrong and Bowie's work is obviously marked by a profound sense of alienation from the very beginning. But it overlooks the longing for love that I see as more characteristic of Bowie's art. It also ignores the fact that the track which follows "Always Crashing in the Same Car" is entitled "Be My Wife" (provided it's not understood ironically as a reference to marital bliss with Angie Bowie). The song begins with loneliness: "Sometimes you get so lonely." But the chorus articulates the wish,

> *Please be mine*
> *Share my life*
> *Stay with me*
> *Be my wife.*

If Bowie's music begins from loneliness, it is not at all an affirmation of solitude. It is a desperate attempt to overcome solitude and find some kind of connection. In other words, what defines so much of Bowie's music is an experience of *yearning*.

Bowie sings about love. But it is often marked by a question, riddled with a doubt, or tinged with a regret. Even when the title track of *Station to Station* shifts tempo entirely around five minutes in, with Bowie immersed to the extreme in the Magick of Aleister Crowley and the esotericism of the Kabbalah, he immediately asks the question, "Who will connect me with love?" And this is *not* just the side effects of the cocaine: "I'm thinking that it must be love."

"Heroes" is a ballad on the transience of love, on stealing time, just for one day. And this is against a background of pain and addiction ("And I, I'll drink all the time"). It's a song of desperate yearning in the full knowledge that joy is fleeting and that we're nothing, and nothing will help us. "Let's Dance" is not just a floor-filling funk track with an addictively sparse Chic bass and drum pattern. It is an oblique and essentially desperate song about the same two lovers that Bowie describes in "Heroes." "Let's dance," Bowie sings, "for fear tonight is all."

The longing for love is so strong that it can also take the form of a demand, even a threat, as in "Blackout," and note Bowie's little nothings:

> *If you don't stay tonight*
> *I will take that train tonight*
> *I've nothing to lose*
> *Nothing to gain*
> *I'll kiss you in the rain*
> *Kiss you in the rain.*

The evocation of love turns on the elevation of the moment, the kiss in the rain, like the kiss at the Berlin Wall, which is then immediately followed by a desperate plea, "Get me to the doctor."

In "5:15 The Angels Have Gone," from *Heathen*, Bowie once again uses the metaphor of train travel to dramatize the scene of departure after the failure of love. The genuinely searing, polyphonic chorus of this torch song is

> *We never talk anymore*
> *Forever I will adore you.*

This is a more elegiac experience of love, dominated by the reality of absence, of a past that is unrepeatable and utterly gone. Never more. This is also the core of "Where Are We Now?," which is perhaps a eulogy to Bowie's loyal assistant in the 1970s and sometime lover Corinne "Coco" Schwab. But love finds a concrete focus in relation to a specific place and time: Berlin in the late 1970s. I am sure that there is some yearning on Bowie's part to be twenty-nine again and move to Berlin with Iggy, to go to endless tranny clubs, puff on cigarettes, drink constantly, and record music all night. It sounds great. But this isn't any simple wallowing in the past. It is an engagement with the memories that often flay us alive as a way of raising the question: where, indeed, are we now?

The closest we get to sheer nostalgia is in Bowie's evocations of England and especially the London of his childhood and youth in the 1950s. "Absolute Beginners" from 1986, named after Colin MacInnes' 1959 novel, deals directly with this period and is arguably Bowie's best moment in the second half of the 1980s. Again, it is a love song:

> But if my love is your love
> We're certain to succeed.

But this is also a love of place, a yearning for England, seen in a certain light, under cloud naturally, amid decay and rubble, like the external shots of a desolate and broken city in Nicholas Roeg's stunning *Performance* (1970). In an interview with

Playboy in 1976, after having been absent from England for the previous two years, Bowie said that Britain needed a fascist leader and even suggested that he would make a great prime minister. These were remarks that Bowie very much regretted later on, particularly after the emergence of an authoritarian leader such as Margaret Thatcher, who was not known to be a big Bowie fan. But Bowie understood fascism as nationalism, which is a complex feeling, one that is much more easily denigrated than considered seriously. Perhaps the closest we get to chauvinism is Bowie's Union Jack–based coat, designed by Alexander McQueen on the cover of *Earthling*, as David gazes a gazely stare over England's green and pleasant land.

How do we live with the kind of memories expressed in "5:15 The Angels Have Gone" without becoming prisoners of the past, crushed by regret, or simply deluded? Such is the conceit of "Survive," which is one of the most beautifully simple songs Bowie has ever written. Addressed to someone identified only as "naked eyes," Bowie sings, "I should have kept you, I should have tried," and then punctuating the end of the first and second verses are the words: "I miss you . . . I loved you." There is a frank realization that "Who said time is on my side? / I've got ears and eyes and nothing in my life."

But this nothing is followed by the insistence that "I'll survive your naked eyes" and then "You're the great mistake I never made."

YOU SAY YOU'LL LEAVE ME

BOWIE'S MUSIC IS ABOUT YEARNING.

Ultimately, this is a yearning for love. His yearning touches something in ours, unlocking a bittersweet melancholy, for example the deliciously painful longing of exile. To be clear—and this is nothing short of miraculous when you think about it—this yearning is produced simply by the sound of words and music coming into contact with our bodies. Particularly in the early work, Bowie's lyrics have a narrative drive and completeness, as with the story of the rise and fall of Ziggy Stardust. But after his adoption of the cut-up technique, his lyrics become much more fragmentary, imagistic, and modernist. Bowie's words become synecdoches, parts that convey wholes but also the holes in those wholes.

Cut-up allows a new way of seeing. It also speeds everything up. Cut-up matches the momentum of Bowie's incredible productivity in the 1970s. It permits an aesthetic grasp of life's speed and shifts, its amnesia, accidental conjunctures, creative shifts, and its gaffes. The lyrical style of *Low* (which contains 410 words) and *"Heroes"* breaks with narrative and commonsense intelligibility. The words say more in saying less and in making less obvious sense. Bowie's lyrics are at their strongest when they are most oblique. We fill in the gaps with our imagination, with our longing.

Bowie hones this oblique compositional technique—imagistic in Ezra Pound's sense—in his later work with great finesse and growing power. In a track like "Heathen (The Rays)," we get a seemingly simple and random accumulation of city images:

Steel on the skyline
Sky made of glass.

Before shifting to a series of indeterminate statements:

Waiting for someone
Looking for something.

Then questions are raised:

Is there no reason?
Have I stayed too long?

And then, seemingly out of nowhere, we reach an explosive climax. Bowie implores, in his best vibrato,

You say you'll leave me,

Before returning to images now infused with a sense of disappointment and loss:

And when the sun is low
And the rays high
I can see it now
I can feel it die.

Perhaps the irony of Bowie's love-longing is that when he seems to find love, the results are a little boring, as with "Wedding" from *Black Tie/White Noise*, which began life as the nuptial music he composed for his marriage ceremony with Iman Abdulmajid in 1992. As he sings on "Reality," although oddly belied by the melancholy lament of the accompanying music, "I'm the luckiest guy, not the loneliest guy." I'm really very happy that Bowie is happy. But I sneakily prefer the music he produced when he was at his unhappiest.

GIVING UP
ON REALITY

WHAT IS THE REALITY OF DAVID BOWIE?

I am thinking here specifically of the title track to Bowie's 2003 *Reality*. What can I say? This is a very *loud* track, featuring the glorious guitar of Earl Slick and the insistent, almost military staccato drumming of "Hello Spaceboy," but somehow it is even more claustrophobic and intense. We begin with an *Aladdin Sane*–like recollection of a random sexual encounter with "tragic youth," which ends up with her "going down on me." We quickly shift in the chorus to a series of seemingly autobiographical images:

I built a wall of sound to separate us
I hid among the junk of wretched highs
I sped from planet X to planet alpha
Struggling for reality.

Although we must always be careful about conflating the song's persona with Bowie himself, the wall of sound is both an allusion to Phil Spector but also to the wall of illusion that Bowie built in the early 1970s with Ziggy. He then hid behind that wall doing copious amounts of cocaine. The ceaseless movement from planet X to planet alpha, from "Space Oddity" to "Starman" to "Ashes to Ashes," is presented as a struggle for reality, which is followed by a hollow, hard laugh, a bitter and sardonic moment of ridicule: "HA HA HA HA." This is what Samuel Beckett calls in *Watt* the *risus purus*, the pure laugh, the laugh that laughs at the laugh, "the saluting of the highest joke, in a word the laugh that laughs—silence please—at that which is unhappy."

The next lines from "Reality" combine a reflection on aging and failing powers, "And now my sight is failing in this twilight," with an allusion to Jacques Brel's ballad "My Death," which Bowie regularly performed live from 1972 onward, "Now my death is more than just a sad song." But these insights are brilliantly interspersed and undermined by two flatly delivered sequences: "Da da da da da da da da da." What does one say about reality exactly? "Ha ha"? Or maybe, "Da da"? The choice is yours.

Against a background of apparent amnesia, the next chorus pulls the song's themes together:

> *I still don't remember how this happened*
> *I still don't get the wherefores and the whys*
> *I look for sense but I get next to nothing*
> *Hey boy, welcome to reality!*
> *Ha ha ha ha.*

The struggle for reality, which is how Bowie describes his entire artistic career, is shown to founder. There is no bedrock reality out of which we can make sense of the world. The more we struggle, the closer we get to nothing. Sense dissipates into meaninglessness. In a very good article from *Sound on Sound* from 2003, Bowie describes reality as "an abstract":

> I feel that reality has become an abstract for so many people over the last 20 years. Things that they regarded as truths seem to have just melted away, and it's almost as if we're thinking post-philosophically now. There's nothing to rely on any more. No knowledge, only interpretation of those facts that we seem to be inundated with on a daily basis. Knowledge seems to have been left behind and there's a sense that we are adrift at sea. There's nothing more to hold onto, and of course political circumstances just push that boat further out.

So, Bowie declares that we appear to have entered a post-philosophical condition. Wheeling back to Warhol's words with which I began, about life becoming TV, reality has become an illusion. Andy Warhol, silver screen, can't tell them apart at all. Faced with the continual pressure of the illusory reality of the media, social networks, and the rest of the bullshit with which we build the walls of our prison ever higher, access to any true reality seems to be hidden from us. All we can do is counter illusion with another illusion, move from their fiction to our fiction, and desperately hold on to the nothing of which Bowie sang in "After All."

Toward the end of "Reality," there is an extraordinary moment when all of a sudden the slightly oppressive, almost desperate, noisy, thumping rockiness slips away, leaving Bowie stranded with just an acoustic guitar, like at the beginning of "Space Oddity." Back where he started, Bowie concludes agnostically,

I've been right and I've been wrong
Now I'm back where I started from
I never looked over reality's shoulder.

If Socrates is declared the wisest man in Greece because he claims to know nothing, then Bowie's position with regard to reality might not be so much post-philosophical as post-scientific, or that which comes after the failure of a positivistic conception of science. It is too quick to identify philosophy with the quest for knowledge. It is better understood as the love of wisdom. Philosophy is that love of wisdom that comes before and after science.

Bowie wrote in the press release that accompanied *Reality*,

> The basis is more an all-pervasive influence of contingencies than a defined structure of absolutes.

This affirmation of contingency has been Bowie's *modus operandi* compositionally and in the recording studio since the mid-1970s and the influence of Eno's "planned accidents" (itself an early title for *Lodger*). But this also describes Bowie's reality and arguably our own. The collapse of absolutes, death of God, or whatever one calls it, should not be met with either pessimistic nihilism or the construction of some new divinity, some superman or *homo superior.* That simply leads to the barbarism of the last century, which sadly shows little sign of abating in this one. If we replace ourselves with the God who has died, then we become heathen, and everything is just "big heads and drums, full speed and pagan."

PLAYING ON
GOD'S GRAVE

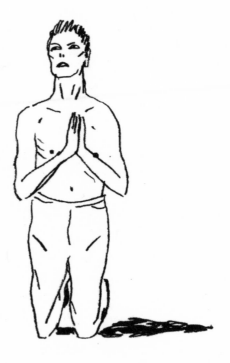

IT IS IN OPPOSITION TO THIS HEATHEN

existence that one might detect what I am tempted to call the religiosity of Bowie's art. God has always played a big role in Bowie's lyrical vocabulary from "God Knows I'm Good" on *Space Oddity* and "The Width of a Circle" on *The Man Who Sold the World*, where Bowie intones, "I realized that God's a young man too."

To pick one example from among many possibilities, the 1999 album *Hours . . .* might be an allusion to the tradition of medieval devotional books of hours, which often contained seven penitential psalms. It is perhaps something more than a coincidence that "Seven" is the name of a track on the album, which includes the verse,

> *The Gods forgot they made me*
> *So I forgot them too*
> *I listen to their shadows*
> *I play among their graves.*

It might sound like fun to play among the graves of the Gods, but maybe it's no game. The shadows can sometimes be long and frightening.

Some of Bowie's songs have a strong prayer- or hymn-like character, most obviously "Word on a Wing," with its chorus addressed to some God:

> *Lord, I kneel and offer you*
> *My word on a wing*
> *And I'm trying hard to fit among*
> *Your scheme of things.*

Bowie continues, revealingly,

Just because I believe don't mean I don't think as well
Don't have to question everything in heaven or hell.

"Station to Station" is the railway journey suggested by the opening synthesized locomotive noise. But it is also the stations of the *via dolorosa* of Jesus in Jerusalem from Gethsemane to Calvary. Bowie's lyrics, steeped in Kabbalistic esotericism, concern the passage between the divine and the human and the possible divinity of the human, which is the entire tragedy of Christ's Passion. From the hidden, supreme crown of God, or Kether, to the kingdom of God on earth in Israel, or Malkuth, "One magical movement from Kether to Malkuth."

Of course, this might just be the side effects of the cocaine. But if one finds a Magus-like identification with the divine in "Station to Station," then God elsewhere can sound downright oppressive, inducing paranoia. *1.Outside* is pervaded by this sense of being watched, for example in "No Control":

> *Sit tight in your corner*
> *Don't tell God your plans*
> *It's all deranged*
> *No control.*

Control, or rather its absence, is a big theme in Bowie's music, which can evoke a real sense of menace. The world is out of control and the resultant paranoia is intense. In the words of "Slow Burn": "The walls shall have eyes and the doors shall have ears."

There is a persistent anti-clericalism in Bowie and an opposition to all existing forms of organized religion, with a particular vehemence reserved for Christianity. One can even see this in one of Bowie's most awful, and awfully over-performed, songs, "Modern Love," where the church that terrifies is played off against the relation between God and man. But this divine-human relation requires "no confession" and "no religion." This line of thought reaches a kind of iconoclastic peak with "Loving the Alien" from 1984 that uses the motif of the Crusades to criticize the political savagery implicit in claims to Christian faith. To succumb to the delusion of loving the alien is simply to make war, invasion, and torture more palatable. One can kill for such alien love. One can even enjoy killing, for it is righteous.

The figure of the corrupt priest keeps resurfacing in Bowie, most recently in the title track of *The Next Day*. This is a point taken to a delightful, mannerist excess in Floria Sigismondi's accompanying video, featuring Gary Oldman as the decadent priest, Marion Cotillard as the whore/mystic who receives the stigmata of Christ, and Bowie himself as the doomsday prophet who suddenly disappears at the end, presumably ascended to heaven. The priest is "stiff in hate demanding fun begin / Of his women dressed as men for the pleasure of that priest." Bowie goes on:

> *First they give you everything that you want*
> *Then they take back everything that you have*
> *They live upon their feet and they die upon their knees*
> *They can work with Satan while they dress like the saints*
> *They know God exists for the Devil told them so*
> *They scream my name aloud down into the well below.*

Bowie is obsessed with the church and priest-hood, I think, because they have fraudulently co-opted, branded, marketed, and moralized the experience of transcendence. As the great medieval mystic, Marguerite Porete, would put it, Holy Church the Great has reduced itself to Holy Church the Lesser. The only argument for God's church seems to derive from holy war with Satan, the Devil, the Anti-Christ, the adversary. Seen in this light, Bowie at times resembles an iconoclastic Lutheran. Appalled by the heathen existence of our civilization and decadence of existing, organized religion, he yearns after a true religiosity, a dimension of the spiritual life uncontaminated by church or state. Doubtless this is what drove Bowie very early into the willing and open arms of Buddhism.

NOTHING TO
FEAR

SOMETHING LIKE THIS DESIRE FOR A TRUE religiosity can be felt in the exquisite, subtle, and densely textured opening song from *Heathen*. Its title, "Sunday," connotes the Christian Sabbath and also suggests a family resemblance to Wallace Stevens's "Sunday Morning," which itself struggles with Christian belief, before concluding, "Death is the mother of beauty, mystical."

He wrote "Sunday" very early in the morning in the rural surroundings of the Allaire recording studio in the Catskill Mountains in upstate New York. Bowie told *Interview* magazine,

I would get up very early in the morning, about six and work in the studio before anybody else got there. The words to "Sunday" were tumbling out, the song came out almost written as I was playing it through, and there were two deer grazing down in the grounds below and there was a car passing very slowly on the other side of the reservoir. This was very early in the morning, and there was something so still and primal about what I was looking at outside and there were tears running down my face as I was writing this thing. It was just extraordinary.

"Sunday" is a hymn, a prayer, or, perhaps better, a psalm, where Bowie ends with words addressed to God: "All my trials, Lord, will be remembered." The song was interpreted as a response to the 9/11 attacks on New York, but all of the imagery is bucolic, with talk of bracken and birds, heat and rain. Bowie, at his most devout and devotional, permits the word *nothing* to pepper and punctuate the song. He begins with the words, "Nothing remains." The kernel of the track concerns how we can keep hold of such a nothing. As the song slowly begins to build, Bowie sings,

For in truth, it's the beginning of nothing
And nothing has changed
Everything has changed
For in truth, it's the beginning of an end
And nothing has changed
Everything has changed.

Bowie simply refuses to reconcile the apparent contradiction between nothing and everything. At once, nothing has changed and everything has changed. But this song is not the expression of some bovine, New Age contentment that everything is nothing or vice versa. This is not musical Xanax. What underpins each millisecond of "Sunday" is a mood of fear, trembling, and sickness unto death. This is revealed at the heart of the song, when one voice becomes two, and Tony

Visconti's bizarre, Buddhistic two-noted chanting accompanies Bowie. Visconti's voice intones,

> *In your fear, seek only peace,*
> *In your fear, seek only love,*
> *In your fear, in your fear.*

While Bowie sings over the top,

> *In your fear,*
> *Of what we have become*
> *Take to the fire*
> *Now we must burn*
> *All that we are*
> *Rise together*
> *Through these clouds.*

In our fear of what we have become, with our bodies wearing the rags and patches of time, we must burn all that we are. Only when we have extinguished and annihilated ourselves, might we then rise up, elevate through the clouds. Up. At this point, the climax of the song, both voices in unison sing an extended

As on wings.

It is truly a spine-tingling moment, which echoes the ending of Stevens's poem:

. . . Casual flocks of pigeons make,
Ambiguous undulations as they sink,
Downward to darkness, on extended wings.

Where Stevens' birds descend, Bowie ends in ascending, most phoenix-like. Nothing remains. Everything has changed.

SUN, RAIN, FIRE, ME, YOU

WHERE ARE WE NOW? I HAVE TALKED ABOUT
Bowie's extraordinary discipline as an artist. He is
a creator of illusions that know that they are illusions. We learned to follow him from illusion to
illusion and in doing so grew up. Behind the illusion is not an ever-elusive reality, but nothing. Yet,
this nothing is not nothing, as it were. It is not the
void, rest, or cessation of movement. It is a massively restless nothing, shaped by our fear, notably
our *timor mortis*, our fearful sickness unto death.

For in truth, it is the beginning of an end. Each
single moment is the beginning of an end. And
death is the mother of beauty, mystical, most musi-

cal. There is no final reconciliation and no final peace. This is why we are restless and scared. But this is also why someone like Bowie, without finding false solace in sham Gods, can go on asking questions, go on making, go on constantly surprising and delighting: today, and the next day, and another day.

Just for an instant, for the duration of a song, a seemingly silly, simple, puerile pop song, we can decreate all that is creaturely (or Critchley) about us, and imagine some other way of existing, something utopian. Such is the tremendous hope that speaks out of Bowie's music. This is Bowie's step, his act of freedom taken in face of the majesty of the absurd and the presence of human beings. Such is the power of his poetry.

Something beautiful and completely unexpected happened on the morning of Tuesday, January 8, 2013, Bowie's sixty-sixth birthday. I got out of bed in the blank cold of the Brooklyn midwinter to find messages from my old Bowie fan-friends, Keith Ansell-Pearson and John Simmons. A new Bowie song with a stunning video by Tony Oursler had just been dropped onto the Internet without any announcement. I watched "Where Are We Now?" in quiet disbelief. The song was number one on iTunes in the UK by 3 p.m. in the afternoon (such is the speed of life). The song is about the past, specifically his time in Berlin in the late 1970s—his most fecund creative period. Bowie himself once admitted that nothing else he recorded comes close to the work of that time. "Where Are We Now?" is an episodic act of memory, a scattering of synecdoches, fragments brought together through the naming of places, like Potsdamer Platz, the Dschungel nightclub, KaDeWe department store, and Bösebrücke, a former border crossing between East and West Berlin. Bowie is a "man lost in time" who is "walking the dead."

I can't begin to explain the effect that this video had on me together with the prospect of a new album, *The Next Day*, whose cover is an iconoclastic obliteration of the 1977 cover of *"Heroes."* The album was released on March 8, a preordered item that silently inserted itself into my iPhone on the morning of that day. Of course, the amazing thing is that this album even exists at all. But it helps that it is really good. I mean it made me happy. Bowie was not dead yet. Far from it. Nor were we. As long as there was sun, rain, fire, me, and you.

Bowie released four videos to accompany *The Next Day*. But there have been no interviews, no announcement of tour dates, no explanations, no media froth. This is what is so beautiful about the whole thing. Bowie has produced sound and vision. Nothing more. Personally, I don't need a David Bowie that appears on dumb chat shows with uninformed and disrespectful hosts, chatting in his best, cheeky Cockney accent and studied evasion. But I do need his music.[1]

One final, recent memory: the other big Bowie event in 2013 was *David Bowie Is*, an exhibition at the Victoria and Albert Museum in London, which ran from March 23 to August 11 and which is now on tour in different parts of the world (Toronto, São Paulo, Berlin, Chicago, Paris, Groningen). The crowds in London were massive. When I turned up at the V & A one morning in early June, the line was so long that I eventually gave up trying to get in. But then I found a way of sneaking in without paying by following closely behind a couple of special

---

1. As far as I'm aware, the only time that Bowie broke his public silence about *The Next Day* was to send a double-spaced, left-justified list of some 42 words to Rick Moody, a writer whom Bowie admires. The list, which functions like a flow diagram for the album, includes intriguing terms like "Effigies," "Anarchist," "Chthonic," "Transference," "Flitting," "Tyrant," "Funereal," "Glide," "Trace," "Tragic" and "Nerve." Moody uses each of the words as levers for a brilliant, illuminating, extended meditation on *The Next Day*. It is far and away the best piece of writing I've seen about the album that places it in the broad context of Bowie's other work and rightly ennobles it by treating it as a piece of serious, consequential, conceptual art: therumpus .net/2013/04/swinging-modern-sounds-44-and-another-day

guests (I don't know who they were, a woman and her child), who were being escorted past the guards into the exhibition space. We looked like a rather older version of the Holy Family as I tagged along slowly behind, keeping my head down. I got in. Inside I was amazed by the amount of stuff Bowie had preserved, even the keys to his apartment in Berlin. I mean, who does that?

The climax of the exhibition was a huge room with a plethora of video material extending around three walls, featuring fragments of live performances going back to the 1970s. The place was packed. Luckily, I found a seat and sat there for about forty minutes soaking in the end of one cycle of videos and the entirety of the next. It finished, appropriately enough, with "Rock 'n' Roll Suicide," maybe from the Hammersmith Odeon performance in July 1973. The song ended. The lights came up. Around me, people were just smiling. Just happy. Wonderful. Oh no love, you're not alone.

I don't want Bowie to stop. But he will. And so will I.

SAYING NO BUT MEANING YES

"I believe in a future revolution in dispositions and ways of seeing that will put all of the past to shame."

—Friedrich Hölderlin

ON THE TITLE TRACK OF BLACKSTAR, RELEASED

just a couple of days before his death, Bowie sings, "I'm not a pop star." For me, and for his millions of fans, he was much more than that. He was someone who simply made us feel alive. This is what makes his death so hard to take.

As the years passed, Bowie's survival became more and more important to me. He continued.

He endured. He kept going. He kept making his art. Bowie exerted a massive aesthetic discipline, created and survived. Indeed, survival became a theme of his art. Bowie's death just feels wrong. How can we go on without him?

Bowie incarnated a world of unknown pleasures and sparkling intelligence. He offered an escape route from the suburban hellholes that we inhabited. Bowie spoke most eloquently to the disaffected, to those who didn't feel right in their skin, the socially awkward, the alienated. He spoke to the weirdos, the freaks, the outsiders and drew us in to an extraordinary intimacy, reaching each of us individually, although we knew this was total fantasy. But make no mistake, this was a love story. A love story that, in my case, has lasted about forty-four years.

After hearing the news of Bowie's death, I listened to him sing "nothing remains" – the opening words of "Sunday," the languid first track on the 2002 album *Heathen*. The song seems now like a lamentation, a prayer or a psalm for the dead. Of course, it is extremely tempting to interpret these words in the light of Bowie's death in the obvious way. Nothing remains for us after his death. All is lost.

But this would be a huge mistake.

As we've seen in this little book, the word "nothing" peppers and punctuates Bowie's entire body of work, from the "hold on to nothing" of "After All," from *The Man Who Sold the World*, through the scintillating, dystopian visions of *Diamond Dogs* and the refrain "We're nothing and nothing can help us" from "'Heroes'" and onward all the way to the triumph that is *Blackstar*, which might just be his best record in thirty years. Nothing is everywhere in Bowie. Its valences flit through so many of his songs.

Does that mean that Bowie was some sort of nihilist? Does it mean that his music, from the cultural disintegration of *Diamond Dogs*, through the depressive languor of *Low*, on to the apparent melancholia of "Lazarus," is some sort of message of gloom and doom?

On the contrary. Let's take *Blackstar*, the album that now has to be seen as a message to his fans from beyond the grave, which I and so many others listened to compulsively after its release on January 8th and then with different ears since the news of his death was announced in New York at 1:30 a.m. on Monday, January 11th 2016. In the final track, "I Can't Give Everything Away," whose title is a response to the demand for meaning Bowie's listeners kept making over the decades, he sings,

Seeing more and feeling less
Saying no but meaning yes

This is all I ever meant
That's the message that I sent.

Within Bowie's negativity, beneath his apparent naysaying and gloom, one can hear a clear *Yes*, an absolute and unconditional affirmation of life in all of its chaotic complexity, but also its moments of transport and delight. For Bowie, I think, it is only when we clear away all the fakery of social convention, the popery and jiggery-pokery of organized religion and the compulsory happiness that plagues our culture, that we can hear the *Yes* that resounds across his music.

At the core of Bowie's music and his apparent negativity is a profound yearning for connection and, most of all, for love.

What was being negated by Bowie was all the nonsense, the falsity, the accrued social meanings, traditions and morass of identity that shackled us, especially in relation to gender and class. His songs revealed how fragile all these meanings were and gave us the capacity for reinvention. They gave us the belief that our capacity for changes was, like his, seemingly limitless.

Of course, as I said earlier, there are limits, obviously mortal limits, to how far we can reshape ourselves – even for Bowie, who seemed eternal. But when I listen to Bowie's songs I hear an extraordinary hope for transformation. And I don't think I am alone in this.

The core of this hope, which gives it a visceral register that touches the deepest level of our desire is the sense that, as he sings in "Rock 'n' Roll Suicide," "On no, love, you're not alone," the sense that we can be heroes, just for a day, and that we can be us just for a day, with some new sense of what it means to be us. This also has a political meaning. Bowie was often wrongly seen, particularly back in the 1970s, as some kind of right-wing nationalist (I note, with some pleasure, that Bowie, unlike Mick

Jagger and Paul McCartney, turned down the offer of a knighthood from the Queen in 2003).

There's another line from *Blackstar*, on "Dollar Days," that is particularly powerful. Bowie sings,

> *If I never see the English evergreens*
> *I'm running to*
> *It's nothing to me*
> *It's nothing to see*

Bowie will now never see those evergreens. But this is not just wistful nostalgia on his part, for they are nothing to him and nothing to see. Concealed in Bowie's often dystopian words is an appeal to utopia, to the possible transformation not just of who we are, but of where we are.

Bowie, for me, belongs to the best of a utopian aesthetic tradition that longs for a "yes" within the cramped, petty relentless "no" of Englishness. What his music yearned for and allowed us to imagine were new forms of being together, new intensities of desire and love in keener visions and sharper sounds. In my imaginings at least, this is how I choose to hear the quotation from the poet Hölderlin that begins this chapter. Bowie's music permits us to imagine a future revolution in dispositions and ways of seeing. In hearing differently, we might be able to behave and see in a way that puts the past to shame.

WHERE THE FUCK DID MONDAY GO?

BOWIE'S MUSIC OFFERS US AN OUTSTRETCHED hand and leads us to the darkest places, the loneliest places, but also the most tender places, the places where we need love and where desire is deeply felt. His music is not cold. It is the polar opposite of cold.

Despite its massive and obvious sadness, Bowie's was the best of deaths. If there was ever the "good" death of a major cultural figure, a dignified death, then this was it. If a death can be a work of art, a statement completely consistent with an artist's aesthetic, then this is what happened on January 10th, 2016. Bowie turned death into an art and art into death. He didn't die a dumb rock-star death at the age of twenty-seven. Nor did he fade out in a fog of addiction, decay and disgrace, leaving his fans to shore together the fragments of a ruined life. This was a noble death in the gift of privacy with all of his fans listening to his new album.

Of course, Bowie's work was about death from the get go. In "Space Oddity," Major Tom drifts off into space, lucidly aware of his reduction to the commodity form, and dies telling his wife he loves her. And so it goes, from Bowie's Scott Walker-inflected cover of Jacques Brel's "My Death," through "Rock 'n' Roll Suicide" to "We Are the Dead" from *Diamond Dogs* and onwards up to a terrific late track like "You Feel So Lonely You Could Die" from *The Next Day*, a love song of hatred, which ends with the words,

> *Oblivion shall own you*
> *Death alone shall love you*
> *I hope you feel so lonely*
> *You could die*

My initial reaction to *Blackstar*, between January 8th and 10th, was very simple: it sounded like a Bowie album. I remember thinking simply and stupidly, "this is really good." Sure, it was jazzy, it was melancholic, it featured new players, but it was in no way a total break with the past. For the fan, *Blackstar* offered the mixture of novelty and continuity that is characteristic of many of Bowie's best records.

I watched the video of the title track countless times after its release on November 19th, 2015. I knew some of the tracks on *Blackstar* already, like "Sue (In a Season of Crime)" and "Tis a Pity She Was a Whore," albeit in different and, I think, inferior mixes (both these tracks are much more visceral and powerful on *Blackstar*). The harmonica part of "I Can't Give Everything Away" was a clear nod back to "New Career in a New Town" from *Low*. "Dollar Days" put me in mind of "Thursday's Child" from *Hours*...

So, what did the knowledge of Bowie's death on Monday, January 11th change? After dealing with the initial shock, and writing a piece for *The New York Times*, I spent the entire evening of that Monday alone, listening repeatedly to *Blackstar*. It simply sounded different, and (although this is obviously absurd) it sounded like Bowie was speaking directly to me. The address of Bowie's voice seemed to have undergone a change of aspect; it sounded uncanny. The words that I had been listening to obsessively for the past three days suddenly had a different set of connotations.

This was most striking on "Dollar Days" and the searing and repeated lines,

> *Don't believe for just one second*
> *I'm forgetting you*
> *I'm trying to*
> *I'm dying to*

Suddenly, listening to the last words of the song, it was clear that "I'm dying to" also meant "I'm dying too." The phrase at the beginning of the song, "I'm dying to push their backs against the grain," resolves into the song's final words "I'm dying to(o)." The words seemed to undergo a shift in meaning as I listened to them. He too knew that he was dying and he was telling us: "I'm falling down." Bowie was also telling us that he wouldn't forget us, his audience, his fans, those who had loved him.

I had spent a lot of the previous two days trying to decode the cocktail of Anthony Burgess's invented language, Nadsat, from *A Clockwork Orange* and the Polari London gay 1960s slang on "Girl Loves Me." But at the close of the day on Monday, January 11th, the message of the song was simple and crystal clear: "Where the fuck did Monday go?" Nothing had changed in the music of *Blackstar*, but somehow everything had changed. Bowie's art would sound different after his death.

This shift in meaning is perhaps clearest and most painful watching the video of "Lazarus." It was released on January 7th and I watched it a number of times before his death. It was powerful. But after his death, the video became almost unbearable to look at. Bowie seems suddenly so old, his skin yellowed and wrinkled, sagging and loose under his chin. He seems so physically fragile. But, besides any tragedy, there is still so much self-deprecating humor on display: notice the cute little show-tune, song-and-dance step Bowie throws when he sings, "By the time I got to New York," and the comedy of his jerkily shot body, writing, hunched like a Kafka character, over an old-fashioned writing desk.

What is he writing? A long suicide note? A shopping list? Thank-you notes for birthday presents? It is not clear. Although Bowie seems to be addressing us directly from beyond the grave ("Just like that bluebird / Oh I'll be free"), he is also still ventriloquizing, still working indirectly, still speaking in character until the end.

For example, Bowie sings, "I was looking for your ass." I hate to break it you, but I doubt that David was looking for your, or anybody else's, ass in his final months and weeks. He is speaking through the persona of Lazarus. The clue here is the repeated line, "Ain't that just like me?" Sure, it is just like Bowie, but it is still not Bowie in some pure metaphysical essence. The strategy of his art is, until the very end, oblique. He just can't give everything away.

LAZARUS,
NEWTON,
GRACCHUS

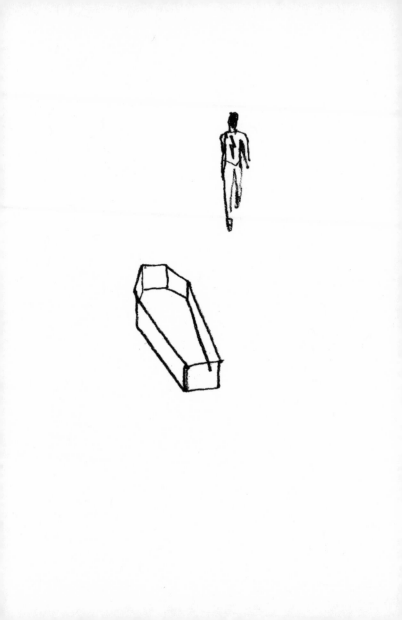

BUT WHY LAZARUS? THE THEME BEGAN TO

perplex me. It was not just the name of his final video, but also the name of the piece of musical theatre that had opened on December 7th, 2015 at the New York Theatre Workshop that Bowie co-wrote with Enda Walsh and which was directed by Ivo van Hove. The show also features the song "Lazarus," brilliantly sung by Michael C. Hall (who does a formidable Bowie imitation throughout). I had the good fortune to see the show twice, once in preview, and again after the premiere in mid-December, when I did a talk-back with the audience and Henry Hey, Bowie's musical director.

The narrative of the show *Lazarus* is a continu-
ation of the story of *The Man Who Fell to Earth*,
based on Walter Tevis's 1963 novel. Nicolas Roeg's
1976 movie adaptation of Tevis's book ends with
Bowie as the alien, Thomas Jerome Newton,
living in New York with a rather serious drinking
problem. Newton hasn't aged and cannot die. The
show *Lazarus* picks up from the end of the film,
showing Newton in his New York apartment,
drinking copious amounts of gin, eating Twinkie
candy bars and obsessively watching television.

Lazarus is the story of an earthbound alien who
cannot die and does not age. The inability to die
is entirely infused with the memory of love for
the character of Mary-Lou, the chambermaid he
meets in the motel in New Mexico in *The Man
Who Fell to Earth*. Her image is projected in
video flashbacks on a screen that fills center stage.
Bullied by a broken mind, Newton eventually
conjures up the ghost or fantasy of a new pretend
teenage girl, who is some quasi-incestuous mixture

of his lover, Mary-Lou, and his dead daughter on his home planet. Eventually, the girl evaporates after being symbolically killed and Newton submits to a full psychotic delusion of lifting off on a rocket ship and returning to his home planet. But it is clear that in reality he is going nowhere. He is earthbound.

For his fans, the identification of Bowie with Newton is total. It always was. Still shots from Roeg's *The Man Who Fell to Earth* were used on the covers of *Low* and *Station to Station*. Roeg had originally conceived of casting Bowie as Newton after seeing Alan Yentob's 1975 BBC2 documentary, *Cracked Actor*, where Bowie plays himself, whatever that means. What is so odd is the fact that Bowie in his last years should take such an interest in the Newton character as to want to re-enact and extend the story. This time, however, Bowie fills the story with his own music, which permits an even greater identification between Bowie and Newton than the 1976 movie, which used none of the compositions that Bowie had written for the soundtrack. The stage show features about fifteen Bowie songs, four of them unreleased, which included "Lazarus."

Of course, particularly in the light of his death, we're going to read anything Bowie did in his final years as autobiographical allegory, especially when given such a series of seemingly obvious clues as we find in *Lazarus*. But Bowie is occupying the persona of Newton, mobilizing it as a vehicle for a number of constant themes in his music: ageing, grief, isolation, loss of love, horror of the world and media-induced psychosis. Newton is at once Bowie and not Bowie. It is through this act of distancing that we are permitted the deepest intimacy.

But why is the show called *Lazarus*? and why did Bowie choose the track with that name for his last video, his final public appearance, his last curtain call? At this point, we need to turn to the Bible. In John's Gospel, Lazarus is the figure whom Jesus raises from the dead after four days in a stony tomb. At some personal risk, because of the hatred of the local Pharisees, Jesus returns to Judea to the village of Bethany, which is now reputed to be the West Bank town of al-Eizariya. He does this out of love for Lazarus, but particularly because of the kindness and faith that Jesus was shown by Lazarus's sisters, Martha and Mary, who "poured perfume on the Lord and wiped his feet with her hair." This is the key moment in the narrative and theology of the New Testament, when Jesus declares that "I am the resurrection and the life. The one who believes in me will live, even though they die; and whoever lives by believing in me will never die." When Jesus sees Mary's grief at the death of her brother, John's Gospel says, "Jesus wept."

Mary, Martha and Jesus go to Lazarus's tomb and Jesus commands that the stone laid across the entrance be hauled aside. Martha complains that "by this time there is a bad odor, for he has been there for four days." But Jesus is messianically undeterred and says to her, "Did I not tell you that if you believe, you will see the glory of God?" Jesus then calls in a loud voice, "Lazarus, come out!" John's Gospel continues, "The dead man came out, his hands and feet wrapped with strips of linen, and a cloth around his eyes."

Returning to Bowie, what is so striking is the cloth around Lazarus's eyes, which is how Bowie is depicted in both the "Blackstar" and "Lazarus" videos. Lazarus is the figure who has been down to the realm of the dead and is brought back to life wrapped in his funeral shroud, his eyes covered. In the video of "Lazarus," Bowie is shown levitating from his bed, being raised up and resurrected, while a demonic young female figure cowers underneath.

In the biblical scene, Lazarus doesn't speak. John's Gospel concludes abruptly with Jesus's final words, "Take off the grave clothes and let him go." Lazarus doesn't say "Hey, I'm alive again; thanks a lot, Mr. Messiah." He doesn't burst into grateful tears or betray any emotion. He just reappears and is allowed to go. Nobody asked Lazarus if he actually wanted to come back from the grave and he does not seem particularly happy to be back with his sisters. Maybe he was happier being dead.

Interestingly, this theme is explored by Nick Cave in "Dig, Lazarus Dig!" from 2008, which also takes place in New York City. Cave sings of Lazarus,

> *I mean he, he never asked to be raised*
> *from the tomb*
> *I mean no one ever actually asked him to*
> *forsake his dreams.*

After his resurrection, Lazarus (or Larry, as Cave nicely puts it) behaves in an increasingly neurotic and obscene manner and

> *He ended up like so many of them do,*
> *back on the streets of New York City*

> In a soup queue, a dope fiend, a slave, then
>   prison, then the madhouse, then the grave
> Ah poor Larry.
> But what do we really know of the dead
>   and who actually cares?

Maybe Lazarus isn't so much the story of a heroic resurrection that proves Jesus's messianic credentials, but a sad tale of someone being pulled back to life without really wanting it at all. Bowie's "Lazarus" is not so much a story of a return to life as the acknowledgment of the inability to die while being gripped by grief over lost love, radical separation from the world, addiction and psychosis.

So, what might Bowie be telling us with the figure of Lazarus? That he is "poor Larry"? To be honest, I really don't know. And what do we know of the dead, really? The biblical Lazarus occupies a space between life and death, belonging at once to both realms and to neither. He is at once dead and not dead. If we think back to the character of Newton – and the naming of the stage show is hardly incidental here – then he is also obviously a Lazarus figure, unable to die, but also unable to live because of the ghosts of the past and the lost love that haunts and tears at him.

Is Bowie Lazarus? Is this why he chooses to use this final persona in order to say goodbye to us? And in choosing the character of Lazarus as the one who is unable to die, is Bowie even saying goodbye? I am reminded of Kafka's remarkable little story "The Hunter Gracchus." The hunter dies after falling from a precipice while chasing chamois in his native Black Forest. The boat of death then takes him on the long journey to realms of the dead, but the pilot stupidly takes a wrong turn and Gracchus is condemned to spend the next fifteen hundred years pointlessly drifting from port to port wearing a rotting, Lazarus-like shroud. "I had been glad to live and I was glad to die," Gracchus says.

Gracchus, Lazarus and Newton are all figures who cannot die and cannot live. They occupy the space between the living and the dead, the realm of purgatorial ghosts and spectres. Perhaps Bowie is telling us that he also occupies that space between life and death, that his art constantly moved between these two realms, these two worlds, while belonging fully to neither. Bowie is dead and not dead. And perhaps he always was …

SHEILA, TAKE A BOW

I WANT TO FINISH THIS BOOK WHERE I BEGAN, with my mother, Sheila Patricia Critchley. It was with her that I first watched Bowie on *Top of the Pops* in 1972 and who bought me a copy of "Starman." She introduced me to Bowie and, to be honest, it was one of the few things we were really able to talk about down through the not so golden years.

My mother died on December 5th, 2015. I don't want to go into details. People say all sorts of pretty uninteresting things about the pain of grief. My feeling in the days and weeks after she died was not just a feeling of aching pain and the inability to concentrate, let alone sleep, but the very clear and very sober sentiment that time had lost its flow. Time just somehow stopped, it wouldn't budge or shift. I felt caught in its nets. Of course, I thought of Bowie's words from "Aladdin Sane," where time's "script is you and me … he flexes like a whore … his trick is you and me."

In the weeks after my mother died, I read as much about grief as my limited powers of concentration allowed. But the only person who seemed to get what I was feeling was the English poet Denise Riley, when she writes a kind of intermittent chronicle about the effects of the death of her son ("Time Lived, Without its Flow"; Capsule Editions, 2012). It's not even that one feels immeasurably sad or that one is engaged in some sort of mourning process with a series of distinct steps. After my mother died, I felt a very clear, almost contemplative, sentiment of time's reality, of being simply stuck in the moment and just hoping that it would pass. It was a state of contemplation that was not in my head. It was visceral. Lodged in the body itself.

The dead give us a grip on the present instant in which we are inserted. We are lodged in the present and it just will not budge. To say *carpe diem* (seize the day) is nonsense, because there is no day to seize. Time has seized us. And this very carnal feeling of time having lost its flow is not lived in fear and trembling, but with what Riley calls a "crystalline simplicity." We are somehow just drifting through time before a bereavement, barely noticing its movement, breathing time in and out. Then death enters into our world and time stops.

Riley writes that this feeling has "nothing to do with 'mourning' as you once might have fancied it. Your intuitive fluid of intuitive time has abruptly drained away. Now you live in an unshaded clarity of bright and dry air."

The present grinds to a halt, the past drags at your feet and won't let go, and what of the future? Riley notes that one cannot take an interest in writing without some feeling of futurity. Stuck deep inside bereavement, it doesn't seem that there is any future. As a consequence, I took no interest in writing after my mother died. I couldn't see the point. The weeks that followed my mother's death were the longest in my life. But I was also incapable of thinking about what had happened, or speaking about it, save for a few banalities and trivialities. I was stuck in a wordless, visceral paralysis.

Then Bowie died. In the morning of January 11th, 2016, my inbox was full of offers to talk and write about his death. Initially confused and repelled, I suddenly decided to throw myself into it. Although I can't say it was exactly fun (it has been more like pulling teeth), I have spent the weeks since Bowie's death writing and speaking to my old Bowie friends and making lots of wonderful new ones. Suddenly everyone was in grief and, in some slightly sick way, it helped. Bowie's death unlocked my inability to talk about my mother. The words began to tumble out. And now I'm writing these words. By being about him, they were somehow about her. What can I say? It helped. I'd like to thank David one last time for this parting gift.

We have to let Bowie go. To death and to life.

THANKS

I'd like to thank all the talented people at OR books for making the publication of this little book such a pleasurable process: John Oakes, Emily Freyer, Natasha Lewis, Alex Nunn, Justin Humphries and especially Courtney Andujar for her brilliant book design. The idea for the book came up during a lull in an otherwise intense conversation with Colin Robinson about Liverpool Football Club. Thanks Colin. YNWA.

Thanks to the following for saying something, often inadvertently, about Bowie that either inspired me or that I just plain stole: Keith Ansell-Pearson, Dan Frank, Jonathan Lethem,

Tim Marshall, James Miller, Sina Najafi, Maria Poell, John Simmons, Anne Zauner. Many people contributed ideas to the writing of the last chapters, after Bowie's death. You know who you are. I'd especially like to thank Anthony Downey, Tim Marshall, Christian Madsbjerg, Rick Moody, Ben Ratliff, Ari Braverman, Peter Catapano, Marissa Brostoff, Johanna Oksala and Gisselle Roark.

I'd like to thank my agent, Nemonie Craven, for making some crucial remarks about the shape of the book. I'd like to thank my son, Edward Critchley, both for love and support (as well as being such an excellent drinking companion). Finally, I'd like to thank Jamieson Webster. She knows why.

This book is dedicated to my sister, Susan, and my family in England.

LYRICS
ACKNOWLEDGMENTS

THE ART'S FILTHY LESSON
"Andy Warhol," "Life on Mars?,"
"Quicksand," "Five Years" *David Bowie*; "The Secret Life of Arabia" *David Bowie, Brian Eno and Carlos Alomar*; "Candidate" *David Bowie*.

WONDERFUL
"Rock 'n' Roll Suicide" *David Bowie*.

I AM A HEIDEGGERIAN BORE
"Changes" *David Bowie*.

A SEER IS A LIAR
"Heat," "Quicksand" *David Bowie*.

HOLD ON TO NOTHING
"Rebel, Rebel," "The Supermen"
"After All" *David Bowie*.
"'Heroes'" *David Bowie and Brian Eno*.

HAMLET IN SPACE
"Space Oddity," "Ashes to Ashes" *David Bowie*.

DYSTOPIA – GET IT HERE, THING
"Oh! You Pretty Things,"
"Drive-In Saturday," "Diamond Dogs," "Future Legend" *David Bowie*.

LES TRICOTEUSES
"Sweet Thing," "All the Madmen," "Candidate" *David Bowie*.

THE MAJESTY OF THE ABSURD
Danton's Death (Dantons Tod), Georg Büchner; "It's No Game", "Up the Hill Backwards" *David Bowie*.

ILLUSION TO ILLUSION
"All the Young Dudes," "Sound and Vision" *David Bowie*.

DISCIPLINE
"I Can't Read" *David Bowie and Reeves Gabrels*.

YEARNING
"Sound and Vision," "Be My Wife," "Station to Station," "'Heroes'," "Let's Dance," "Blackout," "5:15 The Angels Have Gone," "Absolute Beginners," "Survive" *David Bowie*.

YOU SAY YOU'LL LEAVE ME
"Heathen (The Rays)," "Reality" *David Bowie*.

GIVING UP ON REALITY
"Reality" *David Bowie*; *Watt* Samuel Beckett; article in *Sound on Sound David Bowie*.

PLAYING ON GOD'S GRAVE
"The Width of a Circle" *David Bowie*; "Seven" *David Bowie and Reeves Gabrels*; "Word on a Wing," "No Control," "Slow Burn," "The Next Day" *David Bowie*.

NOTHING TO FEAR
"Sunday" *David Bowie*; "Sunday Morning" *Wallace Stevens*.

SUN, RAIN, FIRE, ME, YOU
"Where Are We Now?" *David Bowie*.

SAYING NO BUT MEANING YES
"Blackstar," "Sunday," "After All," "'Heroes'," "I Can't Give Everything Away," "Rock and Roll Suicide," Dollar Days *David Bowie*.

WHERE THE FUCK DID MONDAY GO?
"You Feel So Lonely You Could Die," "Dollar Days," "Girl Loves Me," "Lazarus" *David Bowie*.

LAZARUS, NEWTON, GRACCHUS
"Dig, Lazarus Dig!" *Nick Cave*; "The Hunter Gracchus" *Franz Kafka*.

SHEILA, TAKE A BOW
"Aladdin Sane" David Bowie; "Time Lived, Without its Flow" *Denise Riley*.

SIMON CRITCHLEY is Hans Jonas Professor at the New School for Social Research in New York. His books include *Very Little … Almost Nothing*, *Infinitely Demanding*, *The Book of Dead Philosophers* and *The Faith of the Faithless*. He recently published *Memory Theatre*, his first novel, and *Notes on Suicide*. He runs "The Stone," a philosophy column in *The New York Times* and is fifty percent of an obscure musical combo called Critchley & Simmons.

O/R C